pure
indulgence

More recipes and fun ideas can be accessed through
the Baileys® web site at
www.baileys.com
or contact Baileys direct at
R. & A. Bailey
Nangor House
Nangor Road
Western Estate
Dublin 12
Ireland

pure
indulgence

**Ireland's top chefs and cocktail experts
reveal the secrets of creating with Baileys**

British Library Cataloguing in Publication Data
A CIP catalogue record for this book is available from the British Library

Recipes tested by Alacoque Meehan
Colour photography by Walter Pfeiffer
Black and white photography by Declan Shanahan (except p134
which is by Brian Daly)
Designed and set at Cobalt
Printed and bound by Betaprint

ISBN 1-899047-59-X

First published in 2000
This edition published by
A. & A. Farmar
Beech House
78 Ranelagh Village
Dublin 6
Ireland
Tel: +353 1 496 3625
Fax: + 353 1 497 0107
Email: afarmar@iol.ie

Potted Baileys
Ice Cream Strawberries

Baileys Dublin Bay
Prawn Bisque

CONTENTS

Everyone knows the inimitable rich taste of Baileys Original Irish Cream. It has become the world's favourite liqueur and one of the best-known spirit drinks of modern times. It has been calculated that consumers drink over 1,000 glasses of Baileys every minute of every day around the world.

Most people drink Baileys in the newly fashionable 'on the rocks' style while there are some still who like it 'as it comes'. But there is a lot more to Baileys than that. Its complex flavours can add great depth to food and cocktail recipes.

So Ireland's best-known chefs and cocktail experts were invited to demonstrate how Baileys can be used in a range of dishes and drinks. The recipes included in this book are the result of a nationwide search for the best and most innovative use of Baileys in all kinds of food and drink creations.

Of course, there is an old and honourable tradition of using wine, beer, spirits and liqueurs in cooking so it is no surprise that Baileys really works in food too. Try the delicious Tian of Tomato, Roasted Aubergine, Shallot, Herbs and Irish Goat's Cheese with Chargrilled Baileys Bread, from the chefs at Icon at the Baileys Centre in Dublin, or Baileys Dublin Bay Prawn Bisque from the famous Redbank Restaurant in Skerries, County Dublin.

Although these exciting chefs show that Baileys can be used throughout a meal, from starters to desserts, it is in desserts that Baileys really comes into its own. Hot Baileys Soufflés, Bread and Butter Pudding, Roasted Almonds and Baileys Ice Cream and Baked Chocolate Cheesecake—if you have a sweet tooth, you'll really love these!

THE ORIGINS OF BAILEYS

As far back as the sixteenth century, Ireland was famous for the quality of its whiskey. The traveller Fynes Morrison eulogised it as 'the best drink of its kind in the world'. (By the way, Irish whiskey is always spelt thus—the Scots, who were introduced to whiskey by Irish monks, dropped the 'e'.) Ireland is also famous for the quality of its dairy produce. The warm moist climate allows fresh grass for most of the year, which results in premium milk and cream.

It was natural, therefore, that when the directors of the old-established Dublin firm of W&A Gilbey met in the late 1960s to create a drink that would appeal to the new Ireland, and yet retain traditional values, their thoughts turned to cream and whiskey. Unfortunately, there was a difficulty. Inevitable as the idea of combining these two flavours seemed, in their natural states, cream and whiskey are like oil and water—they just don't mix. In normal circumstances they separate completely. It took years of experimentation before a still-secret method of blending these ingredients to remain married together was found.

The result was a complex blend of flavours and impacts. At its heart is the marriage of Irish cream, Irish whiskey and the finest spirits. Added to these ingredients are other natural elements such as sugar and chocolate, creating a rich and complex mix.

WHERE DOES BAILEYS COME FROM?

Every one of the over 51 million bottles of Baileys made every year is made in Ireland, using Irish cream and Irish whiskey. Long before the ingredients arrive at the Baileys production plant, the company has assured quality through a rigorous assessment programme. Over 40,000 cows, tended by 2,000 farmers, supply the 40 million gallons of milk used annually in producing the cream for Baileys. Every morning fleets of specially designed tankers roll into Dublin where Baileys is made.

All the cream, whiskey, Irish spirit and natural flavours are stored in separate containers. The technique of blending the ingredients is a closely guarded secret, known only to very few people in the company.

THE COMPLEX NATURE OF BAILEYS

Cream and whiskey do not mix easily together. (Unlike, say, alcohol and water, or tea and milk.) Producing Baileys that pours smoothly into your glass as a single liquid therefore requires some energy and ingenuity. The smooth taste of the cream is retained, in partnership with the alcohol, by a secret process which ties the cream and the alcohol together.

Baileys is in fact a member of a distinctive class of liquid that requires special treatment of this sort. Other well-known members of this class in cooking are cream itself, mayonnaise, vinaigrette and sauce béarnaise. A good deal of energy (very often generated by elbow-grease) is required to combine the ingredients for these culinary champions and special techniques are required to hold them there.

Typically a sauce such as a vinaigrette is beaten vigorously to break up the droplets of oil and disperse them through the other liquid; and then an emulsifier—such as mustard in a vinaigrette—is added to maintain the mixture in that state. Egg yolk has been used as an emulsifier of sauces since the seventeenth century. Compared to other members of this special group, Baileys is extremely stable. Indeed it has a shelf life approaching two years. However, combining cream and whiskey in this way is a more or less delicate balancing act, and Baileys must be treated more carefully than other liquids such as wine and stock. For instance, extreme conditions may cause Baileys to separate. It is probably wise, therefore, when deglazing a pan with Baileys to use gentle heat.

BAILEYS IN THE KITCHEN

Under normal conditions, Baileys will last for at least two years before the cream and the spirit begin to separate. Baileys is best stored in a cool, dark place. For occasional cooking with Baileys the half-bottle size is very convenient—though of course a full bottle gives plenty of scope to try the delicious Baileys cocktails and other drinks featured in the first part of this book.

COCKTAILS
AND OTHER
DRINKS

INTRODUCTION

COCKTAILS

The most popular ways to drink Baileys are straight, 'on the rocks', as a shake, or in coffee. The rich flavours of the Baileys seem to take on a different dimension when well-chilled.

When including Baileys in more elaborate drinks, remember its basic components. As a drink Baileys is robust, and can stand a good deal of shaking and stirring. However since one of its main ingredients is cream, avoid citrus or acidic drinks as mixers as these will cause Baileys to curdle. So soda is bad news, as is fruit juice.

On the other hand Baileys goes well with rich ingredients such as brandy, liqueurs, particularly coffee liqueurs or rum, and less well (or not at all) with gin or wine. Its relatively low alcohol levels means that it delivers a great deal of flavour without raising the alcohol content too high.

The essential cocktail is a short drink, designed to be consumed on its own, without substantial food. It typically consists of spirits plus more or less exotic flavourings. An early Irish version is detailed in a book published in 1602 called *Delights for Ladies*. For a whiskey liqueur it recommended steeping aniseed, molasses, liquorice, raisins and dates in fine quality whiskey for ten days before serving. Modern cocktail drinkers like something a bit more instant.

The name 'cocktail' probably comes from New Orleans in the rumbustious 1790s, where one Monsieur Peychaud, a refugee from the French Revolution, served nips of cognac and bitters to his customers in eggcups (French *coquetiers*). The 'cocktail', as it quickly became called, took off, and soon all kinds of spirits were used.

The all-time classic cocktail—the Martini—was invented in New York in the 1860s, as were other favourites such as the Manhattan, Gin Fizz and Planters' Punch. But it was not until Prohibition stimulated barkeepers to invent new ways of disguising bad bootleg spirits that the idea really took off. The 1920s and 1930s saw the invention of favourites such as Bloody Mary, Bucks Fizz, Between the Sheets (better in pairs), Corpse Reviver and many others.

Then there was a lull in creativity until just about the time Baileys came on the market in the 1970s. The best-known products of this era are the Harvey Wallbanger and the Pina Colada. The latest wave has produced the best-known Baileys cocktail, the three layered B 52, and its numerous variants.

GLASSES

The standard cocktail glasses are, in order of size:

SHOT: designed to be drunk off in one. A special Baileys shot glass is available, which is slightly larger than standard.

COCKTAIL: the classic v-shaped bowl on a long thin stem (equals up to 4 shots).

WINE GLASS: typically six to a bottle of wine.

ROCKS: the kind of tumbler used for gin and tonic or whiskey on the rocks.

SNIFTER: the traditional balloon-shaped brandy glass which comes in various sizes.

HIGHBALL: also called a Slim Jim, a tall straight sided tumbler.

WORTHINGTON: stemmed beer glass, ideal for Pina Colada.

SHAKE GLASS: like a small tumbler.

CRU GLASS: long or short stem.

The visual appearance of cocktails is very important—M. Peychaud's eggcups really wouldn't do nowadays! Glasses have to be glistening clean, and ideally taken straight from the fridge before use. We have indicated with each recipe the glass in which it is usually served.

However, the key point with a cocktail is not how much liquid there is overall, but what the relationships are between constituent parts. A B 52 tastes the same in the US as in Ireland or Britain as long as the relationship between the ingredients is kept the same. So we have expressed the ingredients in terms of measures rather than exact quantities. These are not intended to refer to legal measures, but to whatever convenient measuring unit is to hand. As long as the relationships are right, the right result will follow. And of course, there's nothing sacred about any of this—why not try a few different combinations, and who knows, the B 52 of the new millennium may be waiting to be invented!

OTHER KIT

The well equipped cocktail bar includes:

shaker, blender, ice buckets, ice crusher, strainer, spoon for floating, a sharp knife for the garnishes, a flat saucer for rimming glasses with salt, sugar etc., measures, a sifter for sprinkling sugar, grated nutmeg, chocolate etc on the top of drinks.

TECHNIQUES

Over the years a clear repertoire of techniques for creating attractive cocktails has evolved. There are techniques for creating the drink itself such as stirring, shaking, blending, building and floating; techniques for handling that all-important ingredient ice, such as cracking and crushing; and then there are techniques for presenting, garnishing and decorating.

Building: over ice, simply add the ingredients one by one.

Stirring: clear drinks should be stirred rather than shaken (to avoid the bruising effect of the ice), while cloudy ones should be blended to achieve the full mixture of ingredients.

Shaking: fill the shaker half-full with ice and pour the ingredients on top. The ice both cools the drink and acts as a beater inside the shaker. Close securely and shake vigorously; it's time to stop when the ice has made the shaker too cold to hold comfortably. Pour though a strainer. Serve immediately, while the drink is still 'smiling'.

Blending: mix the ingredients in a standard blending machine—use crushed rather than cubed ice.

Layering: gently add the ingredients over the back of a spoon in the specified order so that they float on top of each other, just like Irish Coffee.

Other more elaborate techniques include steeping fruit in spirits and most dangerously, the Blue Blazer, in which hot whiskey and water is ignited and then poured rapidly from one mug into another four or five times, producing a continuous stream of liquid fire. Don't, as they say, try this at home.

ICE

Ice is a crucial part of the cocktail experience. It comes in three basic forms.

Cube: for visual variant on the basic ice cube, add small fruits, (blackcurrants, small strawberries) to the water before freezing.

Cracked: put cubes into a strong polythene bag and biff with a rolling pin or mallet.

Crushed: as cracked, only with more biffing. Crushed ice cools a drink more quickly than cubed, but also dilutes it more quickly.

DECORATIONS

A cocktail is a fun drink, and the decoration echoes that. Typical garnishes include cherries, slices of orange, lemon, lime, kiwi fruit and olives skewered on to a cocktail stick. Red cherries or strawberries work particularly well with Baileys cocktails. Spirals of citrus fruit peel thinly pared and wound round a spoon handle or swizzle stick look good. Umbrellas, swizzle sticks and coloured straws are quick and easy.

To decorate the rim of the glass, moisten with a slice of lemon. Then dip into a saucer filled with sugar (coloured or white) desiccated coconut or salt.

Sprinkled nutmeg or crushed chocolate flake make a nice topping. To get a neat cross-effect lay two straws across the top of the glass before sprinkling.

B 52

Glass: SHOT

    1 measure coffee liqueur
    1 measure Baileys
    1 measure orange liqueur

Layer the ingredients in order into a shot glass—and watch it, this is strong!

BURLINGTON TOLEDO

Glass: SHOT

    1 measure coffee liqueur
    1 measure Baileys
    1 measure cream

Layer the ingredients in order into a shot glass.

CONTRIBUTED BY THE BURLINGTON HOTEL, DUBLIN

DOCKS AFTER 8

Glass: SHOT (makes 2 glasses)

    1 measure Baileys
    1 measure crème de cacao
    1 measure crème de menthe
    ice

Stir all the ingredients, strain and pour. A lovely fresh after-dinner drink.

CONTRIBUTED BY DOLANS, LIMERICK

IRISH FLAG

Glass: SHOT

      1 measure green crème de menthe
      1 measure Baileys
      1 measure Hennessy brandy

Build the first two ingredients in order and then float the Hennessy on top to mimic the green, white and orange of the Irish national flag.
Use a spoon to help the brandy and Baileys to float.

CONTRIBUTED BY ICON AT THE BAILEYS CENTRE, DUBLIN—
THE BAILEYS SPECIALISTS

LANDSLIDE

Glass: SHOT

      1 measure crème de banane
      1 measure Amaretto
      1 measure Baileys

Build the first two ingredients in order, then float the Baileys on top.
Watch it seep down the glass.

CONTRIBUTED BY ICON AT THE BAILEYS CENTRE, DUBLIN—
THE BAILEYS SPECIALISTS

MAD RUSSIAN

Glass: SHOT

    1 measure Kahlua
    1 measure Baileys
    1 measure vodka
    ice

Build the ingredients in order over the ice. Great for coffee fans.

CONTRIBUTED BY ICON AT THE BAILEYS CENTRE, DUBLIN—
THE BAILEYS SPECIALISTS

SKIPPY

Glass: SHOT

    1 measure Kahlua
    1 measure Midori (a melon liqueur)
    1 measure Baileys

Build the first two ingredients in order, then float the Baileys on top.
An Australian favourite.

CONTRIBUTED BY ICON AT THE BAILEYS CENTRE, DUBLIN—
THE BAILEYS SPECIALISTS

SLIPPERY NIPPLE

Glass: SHOT

1 measure Grenadine
1 measure Sambuca
1 measure Baileys

Layer the first two ingredients in order into a shot glass,
then float the Baileys on top.

ULTIMATE B 52

Glass: SHOT

1 measure Sheridans (dark half only)
1 measure Baileys
1 measure orange liqueur

Add the Baileys gently to the Sheridans and
then float the orange liqueur on top.

BAILEYS ALEXANDER COCKTAIL

Glass: COCKTAIL

3 measures brandy
2 measures Baileys
crushed ice
dash white crème de cacao (optional)

Blend until smooth, and serve straight up.
Add a dash of white crème de cacao if desired.

BAILEYS
ALMOND CREAM

Glass: COCKTAIL (makes 2 glasses)

2 measures Baileys
1 measure Amaretto
1 measure cream
ice

GARNISH: nutmeg

Shake, strain and serve sprinkled with nutmeg.

CONTRIBUTED BY THE PORTERHOUSE, TEMPLE BAR, DUBLIN

BAILEYS CABARET

Glass: COCKTAIL

1½ measures Baileys
1 measure Irish Mist
1 measure vodka
1 measure cream
ice

GARNISH: crushed chocolate

Shake and strain into a glass, then top with crushed chocolate.

CONTRIBUTED BY JURYS HOTEL, DUBLIN

BAILEYS FIDDLER'S ELBOW

Glass: COCKTAIL (makes 2 glasses)

½ measure fresh pouring cream
1 measure of Baileys
1 measure Galliano
½ measure white crème de cacao
½ measure brown crème de cacao
2 teaspoons chocolate powder
ice
2 cherries

GARNISH: chocolate powder
chocolate shavings

Mix the cream, Baileys, Galliano, crème de cacaos and chocolate powder with ice in a cocktail shaker. Shake vigorously. Strain into cocktail glasses and sink a single cherry to the bottom of each glass. Garnish with chocolate powder and chocolate shavings.

CONTRIBUTED BY THE BRANDON HOTEL, COUNTY KERRY

DUNLOE AFTER DINNER

Glass: COCKTAIL

1¼ measures Baileys
½ measure Irish whiskey
dash Irish Mist
dash fresh cream

Shake and serve. There's a kick in this one!

CONTRIBUTED BY THE DUNLOE CASTLE HOTEL, COUNTY KERRY

FROZEN B 52

Glass: COCKTAIL

1 measure Baileys
1 measure Grand Marnier
1 measure coffee liqueur
½ measure cream
crushed ice

Easy on the crushed ice, or the drink will congeal.
Blend all the ingredients and serve.
A crisper version of the B 52, and equally alcoholic.

CONTRIBUTED BY DOLANS, LIMERICK

DROMOLAND DREAM

Glass: COCKTAIL

1 measure white rum
2 measures Baileys
dash Amaretto
1 measure pouring cream

GARNISH: chocolate flakes

Shake the ingredients in a cocktail shaker.
Serve in a chilled cocktail glass or if preferred over ice with a short straw.
Garnish with chocolate flakes.

CONTRIBUTED BY THE DROMOLAND CASTLE HOTEL, COUNTY CLARE

GRASSHOPPER

Glass: COCKTAIL

2 measures Baileys
2 measures crème de menthe
1 measure light crème de cacao
dash double cream
crushed ice

GARNISH: chocolate flakes

Shake the first four ingredients and pour over crushed ice.
Top with chocolate flakes.
Another favourite of the tasting panel!

BAILEYS ALEXANDER

Glass: WINE

2 measures Irish whiskey
2 measures Baileys
1 measure brown crème de cacao
1 measure orange liqueur
1 measure fresh cream

GARNISH: whipped cream
2 twists orange peel
grated nutmeg or chocolate

Mix all the ingredients in a mixing glass, without ice. Then add the mixture to a cocktail shaker with 3–4 lumps of ice. Shake well and strain into a wine glass. Pour a layer of fresh whipped cream across the cocktail. Place two twists of orange peel across one another in the centre of the glass. Add a sprinkle of grated nutmeg or grated chocolate.

CONTRIBUTED BY THE SHEEN FALLS LODGE, COUNTY KERRY

MOLLY DARCY'S TERRIER

Glass: SNIFTER

    1 measure Baileys
    1 measure Grand Marnier
    ice

Build the ingredients in order over the ice.

CONTRIBUTED BY MOLLY DARCY'S PUB, COUNTY KERRY

KERRY VOLCANO

Glass: SNIFTER

    1 measure Baileys
    1 measure Grand Marnier

Serve warm.

CONTRIBUTED BY THE HOTEL EUROPE, COUNTY KERRY

BMW

Glass: ROCKS

    1 measure Baileys
    1 measure Malibu
    1 measure Irish whiskey
    ice

Build the ingredients in order over the ice.

CONTRIBUTED BY SCHOONER'S PUB, LIMERICK

EUROPE SPECIAL

Glass: ROCKS

1 measure Baileys
1 measure Malibu
1 measure coffee liqueur

Shake and serve over ice.

CONTRIBUTED BY THE HOTEL EUROPE, COUNTY KERRY

KILLARNEY DREAM

Glass: LARGE ROCKS

1 measure Baileys
1 measure Irish whiskey

Shake and serve over ice.

CONTRIBUTED BY THE HOTEL EUROPE, COUNTY KERRY

BEACH BABY

Glass: SMALL CRU

    1 measure Baileys
    1 measure Malibu
    1 measure Bacardi
    ½ measure cream

GARNISH: 1 red cherry
    chocolate sauce

Shake vigorously over ice in a cocktail shaker until foamy. Serve in a small cru glass. Garnish with a red cherry on a cocktail stick. Drizzle chocolate over the top.

CONTRIBUTED BY ICON AT THE BAILEYS CENTRE, DUBLIN—
THE BAILEYS SPECIALISTS

MONKEY BUSINESS

Glass: GRAND CRU

    2 measures Baileys
    1 measure vodka
    dash Malibu
    ½ banana
    ¼ glass of crushed ice

GARNISH: 1 strawberry

Blend the ingredients with the crushed ice, taking care not to let the banana thicken, which can happen very quickly—if it does try adding milk to liquefy the mixture. Garnish with a strawberry.

CHOCA MOCHA

Glass: HIGHBALL

1 measure Baileys
1 measure coffee liqueur
1 measure coffee (espresso)
chocolate-flavoured milk

GARNISH: whipped cream

Pour the first three ingredients into a highball glass, then add chocolate milk to fill the glass. Top off with whipped cream for flash. This is a long, cold, low-alcohol drink, ideal for a lounging summer's day.

BAILEYS ICED CAPPUCCINO

Glass: WORTHINGTON

4 measures double-strength coffee
1 measure Baileys
1 measure cream
sugar to taste
ice

GARNISH: whipped cream
         cinnamon

Blend the first four ingredients for 30 seconds and pour into a large glass over ice.
Top with whipped cream and sprinkle with cinnamon.
A long cool drink ideal for coffee addicts.

MUDSLIDE

Glass: WORTHINGTON

    1 measure Baileys
    1 measure vodka
    ice (optional)
    1 measure crème de cacao

Build the ingredients in order, with or without ice. Drizzle some crème de cacao off a spoon down the inside of the glass to achieve that 'mudslide' effect. This is the most popular cocktail at Icon.

CONTRIBUTED BY ICON AT THE BAILEYS CENTRE, DUBLIN— THE BAILEYS SPECIALISTS

BAILEYS DREAM SHAKE COCKTAIL

Glass: SHAKE

    ice
    2 measures Baileys
    2 scoops vanilla ice cream
    1 measure cream

Put ice into the shaker, add the other ingredients and shake until the shaker is too cold to hold. Serve in long glasses.

Icon at the Baileys Centre
Icon at the Baileys Centre offers the best of Ireland under one roof, brought together with that special Baileys blend of luxury and playful indulgence. Icon has five different food environments, ranging from simple country cooking to sophisticated seafood, served in a variety of intriguingly crafted settings, from Georgian elegance to the spare modernity of the Mezzanine.

BAILEYS MILKSHAKE

Glass: FRAPPÉ

1 measure Baileys
3 measures milk
2 measures chocolate ice cream
1 dash vanilla essence
2 dashes rum essence

Blend all the ingredients and serve in a frappé glass. This was
particularly popular with our tasting panel.

BAILEYS COFFEE

Glass: COFFEE CUP

1 cup freshly brewed hot coffee
½ measure Baileys
whipped cream
chocolate flakes

Pour the Baileys into the freshly brewed coffee and top with whipped
cream. Sprinkle chocolate flakes on top.

COOKING
WITH BAILEYS

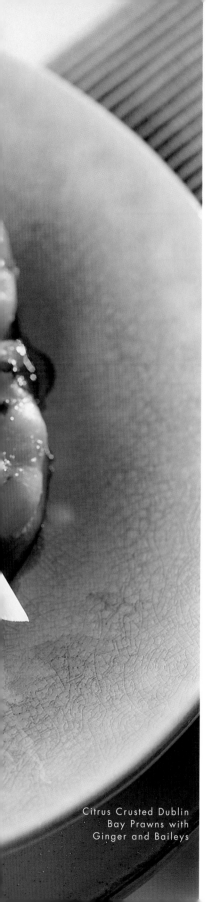

Citrus Crusted Dublin
Bay Prawns with
Ginger and Baileys

INTRODUCTION

As the recipes in this book demonstrate, Baileys can enhance a very wide variety of recipes. As compared to wine, it is sweet and creamy, so it feels considerably more substantial on the palate—as wine lovers say, it has more 'body'. On the other hand it is less intense and varied than an oaky, heavily tannic red wine.

The best use of Baileys is with food with a similar weight and substance in the mouth. It is no accident that the top chefs featured in this book chose robustly flavoured foods such as duck, venison, guinea-fowl and monkfish to match the Baileys. Eggs, vegetables and citrus fruits are less obvious matches (though there are examples in this book of all three used happily with Baileys.) The creamy richness of Baileys makes it easy to use in dessert recipes, though again Baileys does not combine well with acidic dishes such as fruit salad.

BAILEYS IN SAVOURY DISHES

At first sight one would think that for savoury dishes Baileys would be restricted to overtly 'sweet and sour' dishes. Not so. As a starting point, almost anywhere cream is used, Baileys can be added to give that special 'spin' to a recipe. For instance, in this book Irish chefs have used Baileys in a creamy sauce around a delicious fillet of seabass, or poured over baked stuffed mushrooms.

For a special treat, try the Glazed Monkfish from the Odeon Bar and Restaurant which marries East and West spectacularly in a very modern fusion. In this recipe the clean eastern flavours of ginger and coriander are given the taste of western indulgence by the addition of a hint of Baileys.

The key to using Baileys with savoury dishes is not to use too much; it should be thought of as a hidden ingredient providing just that touch of depth or unexpected 'zing' to a recipe, rather than a major flavour. For most meat and savoury dishes, it should be used as a seasoning, like salt and in similar quantities.

BAILEYS AND DESSERTS

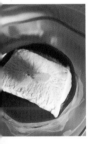

Although the chefs included here have demonstrated that Baileys can be superb in a savoury or meat dish, it is in sweets and puddings that the liqueur really comes into its own. Once again, wherever cream is used, Baileys can be used. For desserts, the chefs tend to use larger proportions, for the intriguing tastes go really well with rich, flavoursome desserts. Try the Chocolate and Baileys Brownie, or the Baked Chocolate Cheesecake for a real treat.

In fact the dessert recipes in this book are the crème de la crème of what can be done with a bottle of Baileys. For the tasting panel the Bread and Butter Pudding from Icon at the Baileys Centre was a real find. Starting with a basic nursery food staple, the dish is brought to another level with the addition of Baileys. It is transformed into a scrumptious dessert worthy of the most elegant dinner table.

BAILEYS BREAD

MAKES 2 MEDIUM LOAVES
2 ½ lbs/1 kg cream/cake flour
sachet/1 level tablespoon fast action
dried yeast
tablespoon icing/confectioner's sugar
pinch of salt
pinch 5 spice or mixed spice
2 ½ oz/75 g/½ stick butter
4 tablespoons Baileys
1 ½ pints/900 ml/3¾ cups milk
egg yolk, lightly beaten, for glazing

Place the flour in the bowl of a food processor, with the yeast, icing/confectioner's sugar, salt and spice. Add the butter and mix for 2 ½ minutes.

Heat the milk to just below boiling point, add the Baileys to the milk and then add the mixture to the dry ingredients to form a dough.

Turn the speed on the mixer up to full for 30 seconds, then turn out the dough on to a floured surface and knead.

Shape into two loaves and place in a warm place to rise for 30 minutes.

Preheat the oven to gas mark 4/180°C/350°F.

Brush with egg yolk and bake for 30–45 minutes.

Icon at the Baileys Centre
Leopardstown, County Dublin

BAILEYS BREAD ROLLS

MAKES 12-16 ROLLS

1 sachet/1 level tablelspoon dried yeast
¼ pint/125 ml/½ cup warm (handhot) water
¼ pint/125 ml milk/¼ cup
1 teaspoon salt
1 teaspoon sugar
1 egg, separated
about 7 oz/400 g plain white/all purpose flour
1/4 pint/125 ml/½ cup Baileys

Place the yeast in the mixing bowl of a food processor and add the warm water to activate the yeast.

Add the milk, salt, sugar and the very lightly beaten (3 whisks) egg white.

Slowly whisk in half the flour until a smooth batter is formed.

Attach the bowl to the processor and using the slowest speed mix with a dough hook.

Gradually add more flour until the dough becomes non-sticky to the touch. Stop twice to scrape down the sides of the bowl—the dough should be elastic but smooth. You may find you have to use more or less flour than indicated above.

Take the dough out of the bowl and knead gently on a floured board for 1 minute.

Put the dough back into the bowl, sprinkle with flour, cover the bowl with cling film and leave in a warm place until doubled in size.

Take the inflated dough out of the bowl and knock it back, i. e. punch it down to its original size. The dough will now be a bit sticky again.

Mix a little flour into the Baileys. Put the dough and the Baileys mix into the mixing bowl and on the lowest speed work the two mixtures together.

Turn out onto a floured surface. Shape into 12–16 mounds and place them on a greased and floured baking tray, sprinkle with flour and cover with cling film or a dry tea towel and leave to double in size again.

Preheat the oven to gas mark 6/200°C/400°F.

Hunter's Hotel, Rathnew
County Wicklow

Gerard Meade

Hunter's Hotel

Hunter's Hotel is one of Ireland's oldest coaching inns, tracing its history back more than 250 years. Menus are based on the best of local Wicklow produce— lamb and beef from nearby farms, locally caught fish, game in season and vegetables and fruit from the hotel's own kitchen gardens. Chef Gerard Meade is a recent arrival, and, while introducing new ideas into the menus, is conscious that generations of customers expect excellent food served without frills or fuss.

Mix the egg yolk with a little water. When the rolls have re-risen brush them with the egg yolk and water to glaze. If you like, at this stage you could sprinkle the rolls with poppy seeds.

Place the rolls in the oven on the top shelf and cook for 10 minutes or until crusty brown on top and hollow sounding when tapped on the bottom.

If you like your rolls extra crusty sprinkle them with a little water after they've been baking for about 5 minutes.

Baileys Dublin Bay
Prawn Bisque

BAILEYS DUBLIN BAY PRAWN BISQUE

SERVES 4

4 fl oz/120 ml/½ cup olive oil

¼ head celery, trimmed and chopped

1 carrot, trimmed and chopped

2 oz/60 g white button mushrooms, chopped

8 oz/240 g fresh tomatoes, chopped

1 onion, peeled and chopped

2 bay leaves

2 sprigs tarragon

2 sprigs parsley

2 garlic cloves, peeled and crushed

4 fl oz/120 ml/½ cup dry white wine

2½ pints/1.25 litre/5 cups cold water

1½ lb/500 g whole prawns

2 oz/60 g/½ stick butter

1 tablespoon plain white/all purpose flour

½ tablespoon tomato purée

4 fl oz/120 ml/½ cup brandy

6 fl oz/200 ml/½ cup Baileys

2 egg yolks

4 fl oz/120 ml/½ cup double/heavy cream

GARNISH

2 tablespoons single/light cream

1 teaspoon Baileys

chopped tarragon

Heat the olive oil in a pot large enough to fit the prawns, depending on their size.

Add the vegetables, herbs and wine. Cook gently for a few minutes, without allowing to colour, to extract the flavour.

Then add the cold water and heat almost to the point of boiling.

Plunge in the whole prawns and just bring to the boil. Remove from the heat. The prawns will now be cooked sufficiently. Do not over-cook them.

Remove the prawns from the stock with a slotted spoon and put aside to cool. Reserve the stock.

Remove the heads from the cooked prawns and reserve for flavouring the bisque. Shell the prawns, reserving the shells for flavouring the bisque.

Remove the veins from the prawns and store covered in the fridge until required.

Place the prawn shells and heads on a baking tray and bake them in a hot oven for at least 20 minutes. This might seem odd but it is necessary to obtain the fullest flavour for the soup.

Meanwhile, in another large pot melt the butter, add the flour and cook gently for about 2 minutes, stirring all the time. Then add the tomato purée.

The Redbank Restaurant
Skerries, County Dublin

Add the baked shellfish shells to the pot and cook, stirring constantly, until they heat up. Add the brandy and light it with a taper. Let the brandy burn off.

Finally, add the reserved stock and bring back to the boil. Turn the heat down and simmer the bisque for one hour.

Add the Baileys, stir and cook gently for a further 10 minutes.

Strain the mixture through a fine sieve.

If you wish, you may prepare the bisque to this point, allow it to cool and store in the fridge until you are ready to finish it for serving. In that case, heat the bisque gently before continuing as follows.

Beat the egg yolks and cream together and add to the bisque. Do not let the mixture boil or the egg will curdle. The bisque will now thicken slightly. This process will take about 2 minutes.

TO SERVE
Arrange the peeled prawns in bowls or soup plates and pour the bisque over the prawns. Garnish with a little cream laced with Baileys and some chopped tarragon.

Terry McCoy
The Redbank Restaurant
Terry McCoy and his wife Margaret founded the Redbank Restaurant in the beautiful fishing village of Skerries in 1983. The local seafood is naturally a prime attraction on the menu, but the luscious vegetables of this market gardening area feature large as well. Equally nurtured by the big-hearted chef are the local millers who supply him with the stone-ground flour for his delicious brown bread and of course the farmhouse cheese-makers of Ireland who produce such mouth-watering cheeses.

CITRUS CRUSTED DUBLIN BAY PRAWNS

WITH GINGER AND BAILEYS

SERVES 4

1 medium chilli, seeded and chopped
3 tablespoons dried candied orange zest
3 tablespoons dried candied lemon zest
1 teaspoon lemon juice
1 teaspoon ground cumin
1 teaspoon dried oregano
3 basil leaves, shredded
1 tablespoon coarse rock salt
4 fl oz/120 ml/½ cup Baileys
20 large uncooked shrimps or Dublin Bay prawns, peeled and deveined
2 tablespoons regular olive oil
1 tablespoon crushed ginger
1 tablespoon crushed garlic
freshly ground black pepper (if necessary)

GARNISH
coriander/cilantro
lemongrass sticks
potato net

Combine the chilli, orange and lemon zest, lemon juice, cumin, oregano, basil, salt and half the Baileys. Let stand for 1 hour. Add the shrimps and marinate for half an hour to form a citrus crust.

Heat the olive oil in a sauté pan and sauté the shrimps. After 1 minute, add the ginger and garlic and cook for another minute. Add the remaining Baileys and deglaze the pan by stirring the base.

Taste for seasoning and add freshly ground black pepper if necessary.

TO SERVE

Divide the prawns between plates and pour over the sauce.

Garnish with coriander/cilantro, lemongrass and potato net.

One Pico Restaurant
Camden Street, Dublin

Citrus Crusted Dublin Bay Prawns
with Ginger and Baileys

Eamonn O'Reilly
One Pico
From working in kitchens all over the world, Eamonn O'Reilly has developed a characteristic cuisine which can be described as modern Irish, but with international inspiration. His signature dishes show Pacific and Californian influence. His restaurant has been highly praised by food writers and competition judges.

MAIN COURSES

THE BRAZEN HEAD
O'CONNELL MONUMENT

SERVES 4

PASTRY
12 oz/350 g plain white/all
purpose flour
pinch of salt
4 oz/120 g/1 stick butter
2 oz/60 g/½ stick lard
2 tablespoons cold water

PIE FILLING
1 tablespoon sunflower oil
18 oz/500 g minced beef
1 medium onion, peeled and
roughly chopped
2 garlic cloves, peeled and
chopped
1 pint/500 ml/2 cups beef stock
¾ oz/20 g ginger root, cut in 3
pieces
Baileys to taste—about ½
tablespoon
1 egg, beaten

MAKE THE PASTRY
Sift together the flour and salt. Rub in the fats until the mixture resembles breadcrumbs. Add 2 tablespoons of water and mix to a dough. Wrap and chill.

PREPARE THE FILLING
Heat the oil in a large saucepan and then fry the beef, onion and garlic until well browned. Pour in ¾ of the stock. Add the ginger pieces. Pour in Baileys to taste and allow to simmer for 10 minutes. Remove the ginger. Cool.

Preheat the oven to gas mark 4/180°C/350°F.

ASSEMBLE THE PIE
Roll out the pastry. This pastry is very short; to make it easier to handle roll it out between two sheets of greaseproof paper. Line the pie tin with pastry and trim, leaving a large lip to fold over the lid.
Pour in the beef mix. Cover with a lid of pastry. Fold the sides to overlap the lid and pinch with your fingers to seal. Brush the pastry and seams with beaten egg. Prod the lid with a fork.
Bake for 25–30 minutes or until the pastry is golden brown.

The Brazen Head
O'Connell Street, Limerick

The Brazen Head O'Connell Monument

TIAN OF TOMATO

ROASTED AUBERGINE, SHALLOT, HERBS AND IRISH GOATS' CHEESE WITH CHARGRILLED BAILEYS BREAD

SERVES 4

16 tomatoes
salt
freshly ground black pepper
8 basil leaves, shredded
1 aubergine/eggplant, thinly sliced
1½ garlic cloves, peeled
2 tablespoons regular olive oil
2 shallots, peeled and diced
6 slices Baileys bread
1½ lbs/725 g goats' cheese, rind removed and thinly sliced

GARNISH

2 tablespoons olive oil, extra virgin first press
2 tablespoons Baileys
2 teaspoons/10 ml dark soya sauce
red pepper coulis
flat leaf parsley, deep fried

Skin the tomatoes: place in very hot water for about 60 seconds, then in cold water for a few seconds—the skin will peel off easily.
Remove the seeds and then roughly chop the tomatoes. Place in a bowl. Sprinkle with salt, freshly ground black pepper and the shredded basil. Mix well, cover and leave to marinate for 2–3 hours.
Preheat the oven to gas mark 6/200°C/400°F. Rub the aubergine/eggplant slices with half a clove of peeled garlic. Season 1 tablespoon of regular olive oil and brush the slices. Roast in the oven until slightly soft—about 10 minutes . Crush the remaining garlic. Heat the remaining oil in a pan, add the shallots and garlic and cook over a low heat until translucent—this will take about 5 minutes. Add the tomatoes and cook until soft.
Remove the crusts from two slices of Baileys bread. Cut into small dice. Take 4 stainless steel moulds and place a layer of diced bread in the bottom of each. Cover with a layer of tomato mix, then slices of aubergine/eggplant, then slices of goats' cheese; repeat the layers of vegetables and cheese until the mould is full. Place in the oven long enough to melt the cheese—10–15 minutes.
Heat the grill pan until very hot. Place the remaining bread on the grill pan until charred on both sides.

Icon at the Baileys Centre
Leopardstown, County Dublin

Tian of Tomato, Roasted Aubergine, Shallot, Herbs and Irish Goats' Cheese with Chargrilled Baileys Bread

TO SERVE

When the tians are warmed through, turn them out onto the centre of wide flat bowls. Then make a pool of the virgin olive oil around each tian.

Mix the Baileys and 1 teaspoon of soya sauce. Add droplets of this mixture, the pepper coulis and the remaining dark soya to the oil pools around the tians. Add the parsley. Warm the chargrilled bread and balance each slice between the top of the tian and the lip of the plate. Serve with sliced Baileys bread.

FILLET OF SEABASS

WITH LOBSTER MASH AND A
SABAYON OF BAILEYS AND DALKEY MUSTARD

SERVES 4

LOBSTER MASH
2 oz/50 g unsalted butter
4 shallots, peeled and finely sliced
2 fl oz oz/50 ml single/light cream
1 lb/500 g mashed potato
1 cooked lobster, shelled and diced
salt
freshly ground white pepper

SABAYON OF BAILEYS AND
DALKEY MUSTARD
3 oz/90 g/¾ stick unsalted butter
2 shallots, peeled and finely sliced
6 tablespoons dry white wine
6 tablespoons dry vermouth
6 fl oz/180 ml/¾ cup fish stock
8 fl oz/240 ml/1 cup double/heavy
cream
4 egg yolks
3 tablespoons Baileys
2 teaspoons Dalkey Mustard or other
mild, sweet wholegrain mustard

SEABASS
1 tablespoon regular olive oil
4 fillets of seabass, trimmed, scaled
and pin-boned—
ask your fishmonger to do this

MAKE THE LOBSTER MASH
Put the butter and shallots into a large saucepan
and cook gently, without allowing the shallots
to colour, for 2 minutes.
Add the cream and bring to the boil. Take off
the heat, add the mashed potato and work it
into the cream with a spatula until smooth.
Add the lobster pieces and season with salt and
ground white pepper. Keep warm in a low oven.

MAKE THE SABAYON
Stage 1: melt ½ oz/15 g butter in a pan. Add
the shallots and cook gently without allowing to
colour—about 2 minutes.
Add the wine and vermouth and stir well. Boil
hard to reduce to a syrup.
Add the fish stock. Boil to reduce by half.
Add the cream, reserving 2 teaspoons. Bring to
the boil and simmer until the sauce has
thickened and reduced to about half its volume.
Remove the fish cream from the heat and set
aside while you prepare stage 2.

The Blue Haven Hotel
Kinsale, County Cork

Stage 2: clarify the remaining butter: melt it over a low heat, then remove from the heat, spoon off the liquid and discard the solids. Place the egg yolks in a heatproof bowl. Place on top of a pan of barely simmering water and beat gently until thick. Or use a double saucepan.

Remove from the heat and slowly whisk in the clarified butter.

Stage 3: add the Baileys and mustard to the warm fish cream. Gently fold the fish cream into the egg mixture. Lightly whip the remaining cream and fold into the mixture. The mixture should be fairly thick but still pourable. Keep warm beside the stove—do not put it into the oven or it will curdle.

COOK THE SEABASS

Heat the oil in an ovenproof pan.

Add the seabass skin side down and fry for about 2 minutes.

Turn the fillet skin up on the pan and place in the hot oven for 3 minutes. The skin should be crisp and the fish just cooked and moist.

TO SERVE

Place some of the lobster mash in the centre of each plate. Place a fillet of seabass on the mash. Pour the sabayon around this. Serve with roasted red onions. Deep-fried beetroot/beet is also a good accompaniment.

GLAZED MONKFISH

WITH FRESH GINGER, ROAST GARLIC, FRESH CORIANDER AND A HINT OF BAILEYS

SERVES 4

16 garlic cloves
4 x 7 oz/210 g fillets of monkfish
salt
freshly ground black pepper
2 tablespoons light olive oil
½ oz/15 g/1 tablespoon butter
2 tablespoons fresh grated ginger
2 teaspoons soft brown sugar
4 tablespoons rice wine vinegar
3 fl oz/90 ml /3 tablespoons single/
light cream
hint of Baileys
2 tablespoons fresh coriander/cilantro,
chopped

GARNISH
fresh dill

Preheat the oven to gas mark 6/200°C/400°F. Roast the garlic, with the skin on, for 15–20 minutes.

Trim the monkfish fillets of any skin or membrane. Season with salt and pepper.

Heat the olive oil and butter in a frying pan over moderate heat. Add the monkfish fillets and fry for 4–6 minutes on each side. Add the ginger and fry for 30 seconds.

Next, add the brown sugar and rice wine vinegar and boil rapidly to reduce the liquids to a glaze.

Remove the monkfish and keep warm.

To the pan, add the cream, a hint of Baileys and the fresh coriander/cilantro and reduce the sauce by boiling rapidly to a thick consistency. Check for seasoning.

TO SERVE

Pour a pool of sauce on to the plate, place the glazed monkfish on top and surround with the roasted garlic cloves, 4 to each plate. Garnish with fresh dill.

Odeon Bar and Restaurant
Harcourt Street, Dublin

Glazed Monkfish with Fresh Ginger,
Roast Garlic, Fresh Coriander and a
Hint of Baileys

BARBARY DUCK BREAST
CRISP-FRIED, WITH BAILEYS GLAZE, SERVED WITH SALAD

SERVES 4

4 breasts Barbary duck
salt
freshly ground black pepper
4 tablespoons/225 ml regular
olive oil

GLAZE
16 fl oz/550 ml chicken stock
4 fl oz/100 ml Baileys
4 oz/120 g/1 stick butter

SALAD
2 frisée lettuces/curly endives,
cleaned and trimmed
2 bunches watercress
2 bunches scallions/green onions,
cleaned and trimmed
salt
freshly ground black pepper

DRESSING
8 fl oz/240 ml/1 cup regular
olive oil
4 fl oz/120 ml/½ cup orange
juice

GARNISH
16 orange segments

COOK THE DUCK
Preheat the oven to gas mark 6/200°C/400°F.
Using a sharp knife, score across the skin on the
duck breasts.
Season the oil and heat in an ovenproof pan.
When it is very hot, put in the duck, skin side
down, and cook for 4 minutes until golden
brown.
Turn the duck over. Place the pan in a hot oven
for a further 5 minutes. Remove and keep
warm.

MAKE THE GLAZE
Bring the stock to the boil. Add the Baileys and
remove the pan from the heat.
Add the butter and whisk it into the glaze.

PREPARE THE SALAD
Mix the salad ingredients together and season.

TO SERVE
Pour the olive oil and orange juice over the
salad and toss. Cut the duck breasts into thick
slices. Place the dressed salad in the centres of
four plates. Garnish with orange segments.
Arrange the sliced duck around the salad. Spoon
the Baileys glaze over the sliced duck.

Lacken House
Dublin Road, Kilkenny

Barbary Duck Breast, Crisp-fried, with
Baileys Glaze, Served with Salad

Eugene McSweeney
Lacken House
Using high quality local foods from Kilkenny's rich supply of meat and vegetables chef Eugene McSweeney offers his customers indigenous Irish recipes, with a constant eye on quality. His principle is 'rubbishy ingredients make rubbishy food'.

Baked Stuffed Mushrooms,
Baileys and Mascarpone

BAKED STUFFED MUSHROOMS

BAILEYS AND MASCARPONE

SERVES 4

16 medium breakfast
mushrooms
1 teaspoon regular olive oil
4 oz/120 g/1 stick unsalted
butter
½ medium onion, peeled and
diced
2 small slices bread, crusts
removed, made into
breadcrumbs
sea salt
freshly ground black pepper
4 fl oz/120 ml/½ cup
single/light cream
8 oz/250 g regular cream
cheeese, Mascarpone or
blue cheese
1 tablespoon Baileys
3 teaspoons fresh tarragon,
chopped

Wipe the mushrooms with kitchen paper. Then peel them and trim the stalks. Remove the stalks and chop them finely.

Heat the oil and ¼ of the butter and gently cook the onion for about 2 minutes, without allowing to colour. Add the mushroom stalks and breadcrumbs. Season and set aside.

Preheat the oven to gas mark 5/200°C/400°F. Fill each mushroom cap with stuffing. Arrange the mushrooms in a wide, shallow ovenproof dish.

Melt the remaining butter and pour it over the mushrooms. Season with salt and pepper. Bake in the oven for 5 minutes.

Combine the cream and cheese. Add the Baileys and season with salt and black pepper.

Add 2 teaspoons of chopped tarragon, reserving 1 teaspoon for the garnish.

Pour the mixture over the mushrooms and bake for a further 5 minutes at gas mark 5/190°C/375°F.

TO SERVE
Sprinkle with a little chopped tarragon and serve piping hot.

Quaglinos Restaurant
Dundalk, County Louth

TURKEY TERRINE
WITH BAILEYS JUS

SERVES 4

8 tomatoes

salt

freshly ground black pepper

2 tablespoons hazelnut oil

4 oz/120 g pinenuts, roughly chopped

4 oz/120 g almonds, roughly chopped

4 oz/120 g hazelnuts, roughly chopped

1 tablespoon sunflower oil

1 medium carrot, peeled and finely diced

2 sticks celery, trimmed and finely diced

½ leek, trimmed and finely diced

2 gelatine leaves

1¾ pints/1 litre/3½ cups vegetable stock

7 fl oz/210 ml/¾ cup double/heavy cream

9 fl oz/270 ml Baileys

nutmeg

1½ lb/800 g turkey fillet

1 pint/500 ml/2 cups turkey stock

1 ½ oz/40 g sesame seeds

Preheat the oven to gas mark 2/90°C/100°F. Cut the tomatoes in half, remove the seeds and season with salt, pepper and 1 tablespoon hazelnut oil. Cover a baking tray with greaseproof paper, place the tomatoes on the tray and bake for 2 hours.

Bake the nuts in a hot oven until lightly coloured. Season with salt and bind with the remaining hazelnut oil.

Heat the sunflower oil in a pan and sauté the vegetables for about 5 minutes. Reserve.

MAKE THE BAILEYS CREAM
Melt 1 leaf of gelatine in about 3 tablespoons of very hot vegetable stock. Whip the cream, add the melted gelatine, one-third of the Baileys and the reserved vegetables and season with salt, pepper and nutmeg.

COOK THE TURKEY FILLET
Slice the fillet. Heat the remaining vegetable stock and gently poach the turkey slices in the barely simmering stock for about 5 minutes. Strain and slice again into fine strips.

MAKE THE TURKEY ASPIC
Heat one-third of the turkey stock and add the second leaf of gelatine and the nuts.

The Barn Restaurant
Glanmire, County Cork

Jean Francois Bernard

The Barn Restaurant

Chef Jean Francois Bernard has a policy of using organically grown ingredients where possible, including herbs and small vegetables grown in the restaurant's own kitchen garden. He finds that increasingly customers are calling for such food, not only because of its excellent flavours, but also for health reasons.

MAKE THE BAILEYS JUS

Boil the remaining turkey stock to reduce to about half, add the remaining Baileys and check the seasoning. Cool.

ASSEMBLE THE TERRINE

Place 4 hexagonal moulds on greasproof paper. Put the tomatoes on the base, add the turkey aspic and leave to set in a cold place. Garnish with a layer of Baileys cream, then with a layer of turkey slices. Sprinkle sesame seeds on top and refrigerate.

TO SERVE

Remove the terrine from the mould and place on the centre of a plate. Pour the Baileys jus around the terrine.

WARM SALAD WITH MAIZE-FED CHICKEN

WITH PICKLED GINGER AND RED CABBAGE

SERVES 4

10 fl oz/300 ml/1¼ cups rice wine vinegar (or white wine vinegar)

1½ oz/50 g/3 tablespoons caster/superfine sugar

2½ oz/70 g fresh ginger, peeled and cut into fine strips

4 oz/100 g brown sugar

14 fl oz/400 ml/¾ cup red wine

½ head red cabbage, shredded finely

1 tablespoon light olive oil

1 oz/30 g/¼ stick butter

4 breasts of maize-fed chicken

20 fl oz/600 ml/2½ cups good brown veal stock or chicken stock

6 fl oz/200 ml/¾ cup mushroom stock or chicken stock

1½ fl oz/50 ml/2½ tablespoons Baileys

3½ fl oz/100 ml double/heavy cream

2–3 drops truffle oil

4 oz/100 g thinly sliced pancetta

4 oz/100 g Clonakilty black pudding

MAKE THE PICKLED GINGER AND CABBAGE

Bring to the boil ⅓ of the vinegar and the caster/superfine sugar. Add the ginger, cool and store for 24 hours in the refrigerator.

Bring the brown sugar, half of the wine and the remaining vinegar to the boil. Add the cabbage, cover the pan with buttered greaseproof paper or a tightly fitting lid and cook slowly either in the oven at gas mark 6/200°C/375°F or on the stove top until most of the liquid is absorbed. The cabbage can be stored in airtight jars in a cool place for up to a week.

COOK THE CHICKEN

Preheat the oven to gas mark 5/200°C/400°F. Heat the oil and butter in a frying pan and fry the breasts of chicken for about 2 minutes on each side. Place in a hot oven for 7 to 10 minutes.

MAKE THE VEAL SAUCE

Reduce the remaining red wine by boiling hard until 'syrupy'. Add the veal or chicken stock and reduce this by three-quarters. Strain through a sieve and keep warm.

MAKE THE BAILEYS SAUCE

Reduce the chicken or mushroom stock by three-quarters. Add the Baileys and the cream. Bring to the boil. Add a few drops of truffle oil

The Blue Haven Hotel
Kinsale, County Cork

Warm Salad With Maize-Fed Chicken
with Pickled Ginger and Red Cabbage

at this stage. The sauce is finished by 'frothing up' for 2 minutes with a hand blender.

COOK THE PANCETTA AND BLACK PUDDING

Grill/broil the pancetta slowly until crispy. Cut the black pudding into ½ inch/1 cm rounds, allowing 3 per plate. Pan fry or grill/broil for 3 – 4 minutes.

TO SERVE

Place a cutter in the centre of each plate, fill with red cabbage and then carefully remove the cutter.

Place the pudding around the cabbage and top with a little of the pickled ginger.

Slice the chicken and arrange neatly on top of the cabbage. Top this again with crispy pancetta. Pour a thin ring of the veal sauce around the plate and then pour the Baileys sauce around that.

MEDALLIONS OF VENISON

ON A BED OF WILD RICE WITH APPLE, OYSTER MUSHROOMS AND BAILEYS

SERVES 4

8 fl oz/225 ml/1 cup light olive oil
1 pint/500 ml/2 cups red wine
freshly ground black pepper
2 garlic cloves, peeled and crushed
1½ lb/700 g piece loin of venison, trimmed or 12 medallions of venison
salt
4 oz/120 g wild rice
2 oz/60 g/½ stick butter
1 eating apple, diced
6 large oyster mushrooms, chopped
1 shallot, peeled and finely chopped
3 tablespoons brandy
1 pint/500 ml/2 cups venison or chicken stock, reduced by half
3 tablespoons Baileys
1 dash lemon juice
1 dash Tabasco
1 tablespoon sunflower oil

Mix the olive oil, red wine, black pepper and garlic cloves. Marinate the venison overnight in this mixture.

Next day, discard the marinade. Carve the loin of venison into 12 medallions and season. Boil the wild rice until cooked. Strain.

Melt half the butter in a pan and fry the diced apple and oyster mushroom. Add the rice and season. Keep warm.

Make the sauce: melt the remaining butter in a pan and cook the shallot gently until soft but not brown.

Add the brandy and light it with a taper. Let the brandy burn off. Add the stock, and reduce a little. Stir in the Baileys. Add a dash of lemon juice and and a dash of Tabasco. Keep warm.

Heat the sunflower oil in a pan and fry the medallions of venison for approximately 5 minutes until rare to medium rare.

TO SERVE
Serve on a bed of the rice mixture with the sauce poured round.

Lovetts Restaurant
Douglas, Cork

Medallions of Venison
on a Bed of Wild Rice with
Apple, Oyster Mushrooms and
Baileys

Marie Harding
Lovetts Restaurant
*Housed in a fine old Georgian
building, Lovetts has built up a
reputation since 1977 for very
high standards, combining
traditional cuisine with innovation.
To keep up these standards,
Lovetts makes all its own jams,
chutneys, pastas, breads and ice
creams. Using as much local
produce as possible, close
attention is paid to the seasonality
of ingredients, while relying on
local suppliers with the same
respect for quality as the
restaurant.*

BAKED BREAST OF GUINEA-FOWL
WITH A BAILEYS AND SHITAKE SAUCE

SERVES 4

2 x 4–5 lb/1½–2 kg oven-ready guinea-fowl
1 pint/500 ml/2 cups game stock, made with the fowl carcases
½ pint/240 ml/1 cup cream
½ pint/240 ml/1 cup medium dry white wine
4 fl oz/120 ml/½ cup Baileys
1 teaspoon Marmite
1 teaspoon virgin olive oil
salt
freshly ground black pepper
1 oz/30 g/¼ stick butter
12 oz/350 g shitake mushrooms

Ask your butcher to fillet the breasts from the guinea-fowl. Remove the legs from the carcases and set aside for other use. Reserve the carcases and make stock from them.

In a saucepan combine the stock, cream, white wine and Baileys and leave to simmer to reduce to ½ pint/240 ml/1 cup of rich sauce. Stir in 1 teaspoon of Marmite. Keep warm.

Preheat the oven to gas mark 4/180°C/350°F. While the sauce is reducing, rub the breasts well with quality olive oil and season with freshly ground salt and pepper. Bake for 30 minutes. Melt the butter in a pan and fry the mushrooms until tender.

TO SERVE

Place the baked breasts on a bed of mushrooms and liberally spoon over the rich Baileys sauce. Serve with sauté potatoes and a green seasonal vegetable.

Pierce McAuliffe
Neptune Restaurant
Pierce and Valerie McAuliffe established their Neptune Restaurant in the lovely estuary fishing village of Ballyhack in 1983. Their cuisine concentrates on fresh local produce, organic where available, and their philosophy is to serve really good freshly cooked food with the minimum of fuss, in comfortable and relaxed surroundings. Pierce says that after sixteen years the restaurant has become more of a lifestyle than a business.

Neptune Restaurant
New Ross, County Wexford

Baked Breast of Guinea-fowl
with a Baileys and Shitake Sauce

MARMITE OF PORK LOIN WITH BAILEYS

SERVES 4

3 lb/1.5 kg pork loin on bone
(shoulder end)
salt
freshly ground black pepper
2 tablespoons sunflower oil
2 small onions, peeled and
roughly chopped
juice of one orange
2 pints/1 litre/5 cups beef stock
½ pint/250 ml/1 cup Baileys
1 garlic clove, peeled (optional)
1 sprig rosemary or sage
1 tablespoon cornflour or
arrowroot

A marmite is a heavy casserole, traditionally in earthenware, with a tight-fitting lid.

Preheat the oven to gas mark 4/180°C/350°F. Season the pork. Heat the marmite or heavy casserole on the stove until very hot then add the oil. Brown the joint on all sides. Remove. Gently cook the onions, without colouring, in the remaining fat.
De-glaze by adding the orange juice and scraping the base of the marmite. Add the stock and the Baileys.
Submerge the joint in the liquid, which should three–quarters, if not totally cover it.
Add the garlic and rosemary or sage. Put the lid on the marmite and place it in the oven (on a tray in case of spillage) for 2 hours.
Remove the marmite from the oven. Take out the joint and place it on a serving dish. Reduce the remaining liquid by half by boiling rapidly. Mix the cornflour or arrowroot with a little water, and add it to the boiling sauce to thicken. Taste the sauce and adjust the Baileys if necessary. Before serving, strain the sauce through a sieve.

TO SERVE
Carve in slices, pour the sauce over and serve with boiled potatoes and green vegetables.

Hunter's Hotel
Rathnew, County Wicklow

Paul Lewis
The Old Schoolhouse
The elegant high ceilings and spacious rooms of this restaurant reveal its age—it was originally designed as an infant school in 1834. Head Chef Paul Lewis has been here for over eight years. His cuisine is classified as rustic modern Irish with a European flavour, using only the freshest and best ingredients, mainly local produce.

PAN-FRIED CHICKEN

WITH GRAIN MUSTARD AND BAILEYS

SERVES 4

4 chicken fillets
salt
freshly ground black pepper
1 tablespoon sunflower oil
2 oz/60 g/½ stick butter
6 tablespoons Baileys
¾ pint/375 ml/1½ cups chicken stock
2 teaspoons grain mustard

GARNISH
2 parsnips, peeled and thinly
sliced for crisps
flat parsley

Season the fillets. Heat the oil and half the butter in a pan and fry the fillets for about 5 minutes on each side. Keep warm.
Pour the Baileys into the pan and de-glaze by stirring and scraping the pan.
Add the stock and mustard and boil until the sauce has thickened. Just before serving add the remaining butter and stir it in.
Deepfry the parsnip for 3 minutes until very crisp. Drain on kitchen paper and season with salt and pepper.

TO SERVE
Arrange the chicken on the plates and cover with sauce.
Garnish with the parsnip chips and flat parsley.

The Old Schoolhouse
Swords, County Dublin

Pan-fried Chicken
with Grain Mustard and Baileys

VEAL CUTLETS
IN A BAILEYS CREAM SAUCE

SERVES 4

24 baby new potatoes, peeled
2 tablespoons light olive oil
salt
freshly ground black pepper
4 baby aubergines/eggplants
8 baby courgettes/zucchini
24 baby carrots, peeled
2 oz/60 g/½ stick butter
4 x 8 oz/250 g veal cutlets
1 fl oz/30 ml/2 tablespoons
Baileys
2 oz/60 g caster/superfine
sugar
10 fl oz/300 ml/1¼ cups veal
or chicken stock
4 fl oz/120 ml/½ cup
single/light cream

Preheat the oven to gas mark 4/180°C/350°F.
Boil the potatoes until just tender.
Place a roasting tin in the oven with 1
tablespoon of olive oil. When it is heated toss
the cooked potatoes in the oil, season and roast
for 30 minutes.
Place the aubergines/eggplants in a baking dish
in the oven. After 20 minutes add the
courgettes/zucchini. The vegetables will be ready
after another 10 minutes.
Simmer the carrots in salted water until just
tender. Drain and keep warm.
Drizzle 1 teaspoon of oil and half the butter
onto a hot ovenproof pan. Seal the veal cutlets
by frying for 30 seconds on each side. Remove
and place in a heatproof dish in the oven for a
further 3 minutes.
Place the pan back on the heat. Add the Baileys
and the caster/superfine sugar. Stir while
allowing it to caramelise slightly. Add the stock
and boil to reduce by about half. Add the cream
and reduce by half again.

TO SERVE
Place the veal cutlets on warmed plates and
neatly arrange the baby vegetables and roasted
potatoes around. Drizzle the Baileys cream sauce
around the vegetables.

Truman's Restaurant
Kildare Street, Dublin

Veal Cutlets
in a Baileys Cream Sauce

Wayne Baron

Head Chef, Trumans Restaurant
*Chef Wayne Baron's basic
philosophy for this city-centre
hotel and restaurant is to present
the customer with the best of
ingredients cooked simply. He
strives for a traditional marriage
of flavours, with nothing obscure
or too exotic, though with an up-
to-the-minute appeal.*

SEARED BLACK PUDDING

BACON MASH WITH APPLE COMPOTE AND PORT JUS, BLUE CHEESE AND BAILEYS SORBET

SERVES 4

BLUE CHEESE & BAILEYS SORBET
½ tub (8 oz/240 g) lemon sorbet
3 tablespoons Baileys
3 oz/90 g Cashel Blue cheese, cut in cubes

APPLE COMPOTE
juice of 1 orange
juice of 1 lemon
4 oz/120 g/½ cup brown sugar
4 green apples, skinned, cored and finely diced

BACON MASH
4 large Rooster potatoes, peeled
3 slices smoked back rasher/bacon
2 oz/60 g/½ stick butter
8 fl oz/240 ml/1 cup single/light cream
salt
freshly ground black pepper

PORT JUS
4 fl. oz/120 ml/½ cup chicken stock
3 tablespoons port

BLACK PUDDING
1 tablespoon sunflower oil
8 slices fresh Irish black pudding

MAKE THE SORBET
Allow the sorbet to soften.
Mix in the Baileys and the cheese. Refreeze.

MAKE THE COMPOTE
Put the orange and lemon juice and the brown sugar in a pot. Boil to reduce to a syrup. Add the apple and cook for 1 minute. Remove from the heat and place on a flat tray to cool.

MAKE THE BACON MASH
Cook the potatoes in salted water until tender. Cool and then mash.
Fry the bacon until crispy. Melt the butter. Add the bacon, the hot melted butter and the cream to the mashed potato. Add seasoning.

MAKE THE JUS
Heat the stock. Boil hard to reduce to sauce consistency. Just before serving add the port.

COOK THE BLACK PUDDING
Heat the oil in a frying pan and fry the black pudding for 2 minutes on each side.

TO SERVE
Spoon some mash into the centre of the plate, place 2 slices of black pudding on top, drizzle some port jus onto the plate, place some apple compote around the black pudding and place some sorbet on top of the black pudding.

L'Ecrivain Restaurant
Baggot Street, Dublin

Seared Black Pudding, Bacon Mash with Apple Compote
and Port Jus, Blue Cheese and Baileys Sorbet

Derry Clarke
L'Ecrivain

Derry Clarke is chef/patron of the critically acclaimed L'Ecrivain restaurant. After working at some of Dublin's best-known restaurants he opened l'Ecrivain in 1989, and quickly won many accolades for its food, wine list and service. Derry is currently Irish Commissioner General for Eurotoques, the chefs' organisation with nearly 3,500 members.

DESSERTS

Caramelised
Pear Tarts
with Baileys Pastry Cream

CARAMELISED PEAR TARTS

WITH BAILEYS PASTRY CREAM

SERVES 4

½ pint/250 ml/1 cup white wine
½ pint/250 ml/1 cup water
4 pears, peeled

PASTRY CREAM
9 fl oz/270 ml milk
½ vanilla pod
3 egg yolks
2½ oz/75 g caster/superfine sugar
1 oz/30 g plain white/all purpose flour, sifted
3 tablespoons Baileys

8 oz/240 g puff pastry
4 teaspoons icing/confectioner's sugar

GARNISH
raspberries
4 mint sprigs

COOK THE PEARS

Bring the wine and water to boiling point then turn down the heat. Add the pears and cook very gently in the barely simmering liquid until the pears are soft but still retain their shape. Allow to cool.

MAKE THE PASTRY CREAM

Bring the milk and vanilla pod to a boil over a medium heat. Remove from the heat and allow to cool while the vanilla infuses the milk—about 10 minutes.
Whisk together the egg yolks and caster/superfine sugar until light and pale. Whisk in the flour until smooth. Remove the vanilla pod from the milk and pour the infused milk onto the egg mixture, continuously whisking.
Return the mixture to the pan and cook over a medium heat, whisking continuously, until the mixture begins to thicken.
Remove from the heat and add the Baileys. Strain through a sieve and leave to cool completely.

MAKE THE TART CASES

Preheat the oven to gas mark 4/180°C/350°F. Roll out the puff pastry to approx ¼ in/½ cm thickness and cut into four circles.
Prick each circle with a fork and pinch the sides up to form a lip. Bake for 15–20 minutes. Leave to cool.

Odeon Bar and Restaurant
Harcourt Street, Dublin

Suzy Pierce
Odeon Bar and Restaurant

Suzy Pierce began her cooking career at the world-famous Ballymaloe Cookery School in County Cork, where the inspirational Darina Allen instills a passionate love of excellent food in her pupils. After Ballymaloe Suzy worked in several Dublin restaurants before joining Head Chef Paul Keaveny in the beautifully restored old Harcourt Street train station.

CARAMELISE THE TARTS

Preheat the grill/broiler to as hot as possible. Spoon two tablespoons of the pastry cream into each of the tart cases.

Cut each pear in half and remove the core. Slice into fan shapes and place two halves on each tart.

Cover the edges of the tarts with foil. Dredge the tarts heavily with icing/confectioner's sugar and glaze under the very hot grill/broiler for 1 to 2 minutes.

TO SERVE

Serve warm on individual plates with raspberries and a sprig of mint.

Baileys and White Chocolate Tart

BAILEYS AND WHITE CHOCOLATE TART

SERVES 4

PASTRY
8 oz/240 g plain white/all purpose flour
1 oz/30 g caster/superfine sugar
4 oz/120 g/1 stick butter
1 egg yolk, beaten with 2 tablespoons water

FILLING
8 oz/240 g/2 sticks good white chocolate
4 oz/120 g/1 stick unsalted butter
3 tablespoons Baileys
2 eggs
3 egg yolks
1 tablespoon honey

RASPBERRY COULIS
1 punnet (4 oz/120 g) raspberries

MAKE THE PASTRY
Sieve the flour and sugar together. Dice the butter and rub it into the flour and sugar. Add the beaten egg yolk, reserving a little for brushing the pastry case, and bind into a dough. Wrap the pastry in cling film and chill for about half an hour.

Preheat the oven to gas mark 6/200°C/400°F. Roll out the pastry. This pastry is very short and so breaks and tears easily. It is easier to handle if you roll it out between two sheets of greaseproof paper, to about ¼ in/½ cm thick. Line a 12 x 1 inch/25 x 2.5 cm tart tin leaving a small overlap in case of shrinkage. Then add weights, or rice or beans, and bake blind for 15 minutes. Remove the top layer of paper. Brush the pastry case with the egg yolk wash and bake for a further 3 minutes to crispen.

MAKE THE FILLING
Put the chocolate and butter into a heatproof bowl and melt gently over warm water. Stir in the Baileys and leave to cool a little. In a food processor beat the eggs, egg yolks and honey together until thick and white. At this stage you may need to re-whisk the chocolate mixture. Fold both mixtures together and pour into the pastry shell. Bake for 30 minutes at gas mark 4/180°C/350°F until just set.

MAKE THE COULIS
Simmer the raspberries in a little water until the berries burst. Purée the mixture, strain and cool.

TO SERVE
Serve the tart cool with the raspberry coulis.

Dwyers Restaurant
Mary Street, Waterford

Martin Dwyer

Dwyer's Restaurant
Unusually, Martin Dwyer didn't start cooking seriously until after he had earned a degree in English and History from University College Dublin. He then worked in kitchens in Dublin, in France and in Kent, England for many years before returning to the sunny south-east of Ireland, where he further built up his experience before opening his own restaurant. Dwyers celebrated its tenth anniversary in 1999, a landmark for this critically acclaimed restaurant.

Bread and Butter Pudding
made with Baileys Bread,
Tempura of Mint and
Lemon Balm with
Raspberries

BREAD AND BUTTER PUDDING

MADE WITH BAILEYS BREAD, TEMPURA OF MINT AND LEMON BALM WITH RASPBERRIES

SERVES 6

7 oz/210 g/1¾ sticks butter, melted
10 slices Baileys bread
2 oz/60 g glazed cherries
2 oz/60 g sultanas/golden raisins
1 oz/30 g brown sugar
5 eggs
1 oz/30 g caster/superfine sugar
7 fl oz/210 ml /¾ cup milk
¾ pint/375 ml/1½ cups single/light cream
vanilla pod, split lengthways
6 tablespoons Baileys

TEMPURA

7 oz/210 g plain white/all purpose flour
1 oz/30 g icing/confectioner's sugar
1 pint/500 ml/2 cups water
18 lemon balm leaves
18 mint leaves

GARNISH

1 punnet (4 oz/120 g) raspberries
6 tablespoons Baileys
6 tablespoons crème anglaise
icing/confectioner's sugar, to dust

Preheat the oven to gas mark 4/180°C/350°F. Brush a deep ovenproof dish with some of the butter. Dip the slices of bread in the remaining melted butter and make a layer on the bottom of the dish. Sprinkle some cherries, sultanas and a little brown sugar over the bread and cover with more bread dipped in butter. Continue until all the fruit and bread is used up. Whisk the eggs and caster/superfine sugar together in a bowl.

Place the milk and cream in a pan and bring to the boil with the vanilla pod. Remove the pod from the milk and add the Baileys slowly to the milk. Slowly add the milk mixture to the egg mixture stirring all the time. Pour the mixture over the pudding and sprinkle with a little brown sugar. Place the dish in a baking tray filled with water to a depth of about 1 inch/2 cm. Bake for 30–45 minutes.

MAKE THE TEMPURA
Mix the flour and icing/confectioner's sugar together. Slowly add water until the right consistency is achieved, like a thick batter. Rub the lemon balm leaves with your thumb then dip in the tempura. Deep fry until crisp. Repeat with the mint leaves.

TO SERVE
Using a pastry cutter, cut out a portion of the pudding and place in the centre of the plate. Arrange the tempura around the pudding and sprinkle with raspberries. Dribble Baileys and crème anglaise around the plate. Dust with icing/confectioner's sugar.

Icon at the Baileys Centre
Leopardstown, County Dublin

CHOCOLATE AND BAILEYS BROWNIE

WITH RASPBERRY SORBET

SERVES 6

SORBET
1 pint/500 ml/2 cups water
9 oz/270 g caster/superfine sugar
1 punnet (4 oz/120 g) raspberries

BROWNIE
2½ oz/70 g plain white/all
purpose flour
2½ oz/70 g cocoa
10 oz/300 g dark/semi-sweet
chocolate (75% cocoa solids)
4 eggs
7 oz/210 g caster/superfine sugar
8 oz/240 g/2 sticks unsalted butter
3 tablespoons Baileys

MAKE THE SORBET
Boil the water, sugar and raspberries together, then blend in a liquidiser or blender.
If you have an ice cream machine, churn until frozen. If not, place in a freezer and stir every 20 minutes until frozen.

MAKE THE BROWNIE
Preheat the oven to gas mark 4/180°C/350°F.
Sieve the flour and cocoa onto a plate.
Melt the chocolate in a bowl over a pot of hot water.
Beat the eggs and sugar together in a processor.
Melt the butter and add it to the egg mixture.
Add the flour and cocoa to the butter and egg mixture. Add half of the Baileys to the mixture.
Stir in the melted chocolate.
Pour into a greased brownie tin. Bake for 30 minutes. Allow to cool then brush with the remaining Baileys.

TO SERVE
Slice the brownie into squares and sprinkle with cocoa powder. Serve slightly warm with a ball of raspberry sorbet.

The Blue Haven Hotel
Kinsale, County Cork

Chocolate and
Baileys Brownie
Sorbet

The Blue Haven Hotel, Kinsale, Co Cork
*In the middle of the 'gourmet capital of Ireland'
lies the Blue Haven Hotel, one of the founders
of the Kinsale Good Food Circle. Its cuisine is
famous for locally caught shellfish and other
seafood of the highest quality. Baileys Ice
Cream is an exceptionally popular dessert.*

Baileys Nougat Glacé

BAILEYS NOUGAT GLACÉ

SERVES 4

5 oz/150 g dried grapes, diced
5 oz/150 g fruit confit (pineapple,
cherries, oranges etc), cubed
3 fl oz/90 ml/6 tablespoons
Baileys
5 oz/150 g praline
4 gelatine leaves
4 oz/120 g sugar
4 oz/120 g glucose
7 oz/210 g honey
8 egg whites
1 ¾ pints/1 litre/3½ cups
double/heavy cream

BAILEYS SAUCE
8 fl oz/240 ml/1 cup milk
1½ teaspoons instant custard
powder
3 tablespoons Baileys

MAKE THE NOUGAT GLACÉ
Soak the fruits in the Baileys.
Break the praline into small pieces. Place the
gelatine leaves in a little water to melt.
Place the sugar, glucose and honey in a saucepan
and mix well. Add a little water and heat to
121° or bring to the boil and boil for 2 minutes.
Whisk the egg whites and while whisking add
the sugar, glucose and honey mix. Squeeze out
the gelatine and add to the mixture. Allow this
meringue mixture to cool.
Whip the cream and combine with the
meringue, infused fruits and praline pieces.
Place in a terrine dish about 6 inches/10 cm
deep and refrigerate. Alternatively, this nougat
glacé can be frozen in which case omit the
gelatine.

MAKE THE BAILEYS SAUCE
Make the custard according to instructions.
When cool add the Baileys.

TO SERVE
Remove from the mould and cut into slices.
Serve accompanied by the sauce.

The Barn Restaurant
Glanmire, County Cork

HOT BAILEYS SOUFFLÉS

SERVES 6

12 small pieces of plain sponge or
Madeira cake
12 tablespoons Baileys
3 fl oz/90 ml pastry cream
2 egg yolks
3 egg whites
½ teaspoon lemon juice
1 oz/15 g caster/superfine sugar
1 oz/30 g/¼ stick butter

Soak the cake slices in the Baileys.

Preheat the oven to gas mark 6/200°C/400°F.

Combine the pastry cream and egg yolks together.

Whisk the egg whites to a soft peak. Add the lemon juice and half the sugar and whisk to the ribbon stage.

Fold the meringue into the pastry cream.

Grease six ramekin dishes with butter then coat them in the remaining sugar.

Pour half the mixture into the dishes then add the soaked sponge. Pour in more mixture.

Bake the soufflés for 8–10 minutes. Serve immediately.

Denis Lenihan
Ashford Castle
Employing twenty chefs in its kitchen, and winner of innumerable awards for its food, Ashford Castle in County Mayo is one of Ireland's best-known restaurants. All food is bought within a twenty-five mile radius of the castle. Salmon is fished from the local river, and over half of the vegetables are organically grown.

Ashford Castle
Cong, County Mayo

ROASTED ALMONDS AND BAILEYS ICE CREAM

SERVES 6

8 oz/250 g/1 cup almond flakes
1¾ pints/1 litre/3½ cups double/heavy cream
6 tablespoons icing/confectioner's sugar
1 tablespoon instant coffee
5 fl oz/10 tablespoons/½ cup Baileys

GARNISH
icing/confectioner's sugar
finger biscuits

Roast the almonds: place in a dry pan over a medium heat and cook until golden. Allow to cool.

Half whip the cream and while doing so add the almonds, sugar, coffee and Baileys in the order listed.

Whip the mixture to just before it becomes firm.

Place in plastic containers and freeze.

TO SERVE
Place scoops of ice cream on individual plates and dust with icing/confectioner's sugar. Serve some finger biscuits on the side.

Annie's Restaurant
Ballydehob, County Cork

Roasted Almonds and
Baileys Ice Cream

Anne Barry
Annie's Restaurant
Freshness and simplicity in cooking has been the key to the success of this tiny, village restaurant for over sixteen years. It's so small that patrons have to have their pre-meal drink in the local pub! Everything is freshly made on the day, using local ingredients—fish is delivered every night, meat comes from the local butcher, farmhouse cheeses are local and all the breads, ice creams and desserts are made up on the premises. Baileys Ice Cream has been the first choice on the dessert menu since 1983, and no one has ever dared take it off.

Trio of Baileys
Cream Desserts

TRIO OF BAILEYS CREAM DESSERTS

SERVES 4

WHITE CHOCOLATE MOUSSE
4 leaves of gelatine
8 oz/240 g white chocolate
3 whole eggs
1 pint/500 ml double/heavy cream, whipped
2 tablespoons Baileys

BAILEYS ICE CREAM
2 pints/1 litre single/light cream
¼ pint/250 ml milk
1 vanilla pod, split and seeds scraped out
3 egg yolks
2 oz/60 g caster/superfine sugar
3 tablespoons Baileys

BAILEYS CHOCOLATE MARQUISE
4 eggs, separated
2 oz/60 g cocoa powder
3 oz/90g caster/superfine sugar

WHITE CHOCOLATE MOUSSE
Soak the gelatine leaves in cold water.
Place the chocolate in a bowl over warm water and melt.
Break the eggs into a basin over simmering water and whisk until frothy. Squeeze out the gelatine and whisk into the eggs.
Next, stir in the melted white chocolate, add the cream and the Baileys, whisk well and place in the refrigerator to set.

BAILEYS ICE CREAM
Place the cream, milk and the skin from the vanilla pod in a saucepan and bring to the boil. Place the egg yolks, sugar, vanilla seeds and Baileys in a basin and whisk.
Pour the heated cream and milk mixture onto the egg yolk mixture and whisk well. Place on a low heat and cook until the mixture coats the back of a spoon. Pass through a sieve. Chill the mixture. Churn it in an ice cream machine and then place it in the freezer.

BAILEYS CHOCOLATE MARQUISE
Preheat the oven to gas mark 6/200°C/400°F.
Place the egg yolks in a basin and whisk in the cocoa powder and one-third of the caster/superfine sugar. Mix well.
Whisk the egg whites until stiff. Add the remaining sugar and whisk well.
Fold the egg yolk mixture into the meringue mixture. Spread on a non-stick tray and bake for 10 minutes. Remove and allow to cool.

MacNean Bistro
Blacklion, County Cavan

DARK CHOCOLATE MOUSSE

4 oz/120 g dark bitter/semi-
sweet chocolate
5 oz/150 g/1¼ sticks butter
8 fl oz/250 ml double/heavy
cream, whipped
3 oz/90 g cocoa powder
4 eggs, separated
4 oz/120 g caster/superfine
sugar
4 leaves gelatine, soaked in
cold water
1 tablespoon Baileys

RASPBERRY COULIS

8 oz/240 g raspberries
½ pint/250 ml stock syrup
1 oz/30 g icing/confectioner's
sugar
squeeze lemon juice
dark chocolate

GARNISHES

4 tuiles
spun sugar
mint leaves
fresh fruit
icing/confectioner's sugar, for
dusting

DARK CHOCOLATE MOUSSE

Place the chocolate in a bowl over warm water and melt.

Melt the butter and add the cream and cocoa powder.

Whisk the egg yolks with half the caster/superfine sugar. Add the melted chocolate.

Dissolve the gelatine in a little boiling water. Add to the chocolate mixture.

Beat the egg whites until stiff. Add the remaining caster/superfine sugar and beat until the mixture is shiny and glossy.

Whisk the cream and butter into the chocolate mixture. Fold the egg white mixture and Baileys into the chocolate mixture.

RASPBERRY COULIS

Place all the ingredients in a food processor and blend until smooth. Pass through a fine sieve and then chill.

TO ASSEMBLE THE ROULADE OF MARQUISE AND CHOCOLATE MOUSSE

Oil a terrine mould, and then line it with cling film. Cut a slice of marquise to fill the base. Spoon a layer of the dark chocolate mousse mixture on top of the marquise.

Place a slice of marquise on top of the mousse, and then add a layer of mousse. Place in the refrigerator to chill and set.

TO SERVE

For each individual serving take a circle cutter, cut a circle from the roulade and place in the centre of a plate. Place a scoop of ice cream in a tuile. Place beside the roulade.

Pipe some Baileys white chocolate mousse into a chocolate tear drop and place on the plate beside the other desserts to form a triangle.

Drizzle some raspberry coulis around the edge of the plate and garnish with spun sugar, mint and fresh fruit. Dust with icing/confectioner's sugar.

Neven Maguire
MacNean Bistro
Neven Maguire's family restaurant is a magnet for food lovers in the area. Serving classic and innovative dishes in an intimate and friendly family-style dining-room, a warm welcome is guaranteed. An enthusiastic and hardworking chef, his special concern is to create dishes in which the taste of locally produced organic ingredients is equalled by their visual appeal.

BAILEYS PARFAIT

SERVES 4

5 large egg whites
5 oz/150 g/10 tablespoons
caster/superfine sugar
1 pint/500 ml double/heavy
cream
2 egg yolks
9 tablespoons Baileys

GARNISH
fruit coulis

Whip the egg whites with four-fifths of the sugar until glossy. Whip the cream in another bowl. In a third bowl whip the egg yolks with the remaining sugar and the Baileys to a creamy consistency. Line an oblong tin with cling film. Carefully fold the three mixtures together and place in the tin. Freeze for 6 hours or preferably overnight.

Serve cut in slices with the fruit coulis of your choice.

Pat Moore
Beginish Restaurant
Pat Moore became a restaurateur late in life, after her children had completed their education and left home. After extensive experience in Paris, Zurich and England, she opened the Beginish Restaurant, which quickly became a favourite in Dingle, a town that rivals Kinsale in County Cork for its cuisine and variety of restaurants.

Beginish Restaurant
Dingle, County Kerry

Baileys Parfait

POTTED BAILEYS ICE CREAM STRAWBERRIES

SERVES 4

BAILEYS ICE CREAM
6 egg yolks
4 oz/120 g caster/superfine sugar
1 pint/500 ml/2 cups single/light cream
1 pint/500 ml/2 cups milk
6 tablespoons Baileys

BAILEYS SABAYON
5 egg yolks
1½ tablespoons Baileys
5 oz/150 g sugar
2 tablespoons water
1 small punnet (4 oz/125 g) strawberries

MAKE THE ICE CREAM

Mix the egg yolks and sugar together until dissolved.
Boil the cream and milk together.
Add the cream and milk to the egg mixture. Mix thoroughly.
Return to the pot and heat slowly on a low heat until the mixture thickens slightly, being careful not to boil.
Place in a clean mixing bowl, mix in the Baileys and leave to cool.
Churn in an ice cream machine or freeze and stir every 20 minutes until set.

MAKE THE SABAYON

Place the egg yolks and Baileys in a food processor and whisk on a high setting.
Heat the sugar and water to the hard boil stage—130°C/250°F if you are using a sugar thermometer—or to the soft ball stage, when a drop added to a glass of water forms a soft ball.
Slowly add the sugar mixture to the egg mixture while mixing. Reserve until ready to assemble the potted strawberries.

POT THE ICE CREAM AND STRAWBERRIES

Preheat the grill or broiler to as hot as possible, or have a blow torch ready.
Put 2 scoops of Baileys ice cream into each of 4 ramekins.
Then place 5 halved strawberries on top of the ice cream.
Spoon Baileys sabayon on top of the strawberries, covering the strawberries completely.
Place under the grill/broiler to brown or use a blow torch to brown the surfaces.
Serve immediately.

The Blue Haven Hotel
Kinsale, County Cork

Potted Baileys
Ice Cream Strawberries

Pat Kerley
Quaglinos
*After training in the West End of London and in France
and Switzerland, chef/proprietor Pat Kerley opened his
award-winning restaurant in 1987. Like many of his
fellow chefs he is anxious to use as much local
organically grown produce as possible; unusually, he
combines modern Irish cooking with an Italian focus. As
a classic cook he is delighted to see the resurgence of
classical cookery with a new attention to lighter sauces,
less flour and a modern presentation.*

Individual Baileys
Semi Fredo

INDIVIDUAL BAILEYS SEMI FREDO

SERVES 4

3 eggs, separated
6 oz/180 g sugar
juice of half a lemon
4 fl oz/120 ml stock syrup
2 tablespoons cold water
6 fl oz/180 ml Baileys
4 fl oz/100 ml/½ cup double/
heavy cream, semi-whipped
4 oz/120 g Amaretti biscuits

MAKE THE MERINGUE
Whisk the egg whites to soft peaks. Gradually add the sugar and the lemon juice. Whisk until firm. Set aside.

MAKE THE SABAYON
Heat the syrup. Combine 2 tablespoons of cold water and the egg yolks. Whisk in a food processor at medium speed for about 5 minutes until the mixture is 4–5 times the original volume.
Gradually pour in the hot stock syrup and beat at high speed for 2 minutes. Cool the sabayon by continuing to beat at low speed for about 10 minutes. Fold in the Baileys, the cream and lastly the meringue mixture (do not over mix).

TO ASSEMBLE
Take 4 stainless steel ring moulds. Seal the outside bottom of the moulds with tin foil. Line with cling film.
Lightly crush the Amaretti biscuits, reserving some for the garnish. Cover the bottom of the moulds with the biscuits. Fill the moulds with the mousse mixture and freeze.

TO SERVE
Remove from the freezer and turn out on to the centre of plates. Garnish with Amaretti biscuits.

Quaglinos Restaurant
Dundalk, County Louth

BAILEYS BAKED ALASKA

SERVES 4

3–4 tablespoons ground almonds
4 scoops Baileys ice cream
4 square Madeira cake slices
½ inch/1 cm thick
2–3 tablespoons brandy
9–12 mandarin segments
3 egg whites
6 oz/180 g light muscovado
sugar

GARNISH
icing/confectioner's sugar, for
dusting
12 mandarin segments

Place the almonds on a plate and roll the ice cream scoops in them. Place on a baking sheet and freeze for 30 minutes until firm.

Place the cake slices well apart on a baking sheet. Drizzle with brandy and arrange the mandarin segments end-to-end to make a ring in the centre of each slice.

Place an almond-covered ice cream scoop in the middle of each ring. Return to the freezer while you make the meringue.

Pre-heat the oven to gas mark 8/230°C/450°F.

Place the egg whites in a clean, grease-free bowl. Whisk in the sugar, a tablespoon at a time, whisking thoroughly after each addition until the mixture forms soft peaks.

Remove the cake slices and ice cream from the freezer. Spoon the meringue over the ice cream and spread to cover.

Bake for about 5 minutes until the meringue starts to brown.

TO SERVE
Transfer to serving plates. Dust with icing/confectioner's sugar, garnish with mandarin segments and serve immediately.

Icon at the Baileys Centre
Leopardstown, County Dublin

Baileys Baked Chocolate Cheesecake

BAILEYS BAKED CHOCOLATE CHEESECAKE

SERVES 6

FOR THE BASE
4 oz/110 g sweet oat biscuits/cookies
2 oz/50 g hazelnuts, toasted and chopped
1 oz/25 g butter, melted

FOR THE FILLING
3½ oz/100 g dark continental/semi-sweet chocolate (75% cocoa)
9 oz/250 g Mascarpone cream cheese
7 oz/200 g fromage frais (8% fat)
2 large eggs
1½ oz/40 g caster/superfine sugar
2 tablespoons Baileys
2 oz/50 g raisins (optional)
4 oz/110 g whole toasted hazelnuts (optional)

GARNISH
3½ oz/100 g dark continental/semi-sweet chocolate (75% cocoa)
cocoa powder
crème fraîche or cream

Preheat the oven to gas mark 6/200°C/400°F.
Crush the biscuits with a rolling pin, not too finely.
Add the chopped nuts and melted butter, and mix everything very thoroughly.
Press the mixture firmly into the base of a 7 inch/18 cm cake tin with 3 inch/7.5 cm high sides. Bake for 20 minutes then remove from the oven and cool.
Reduce the oven to gas mark 2/150°C/300°F.
Melt the chocolate in a bowl over a pan of hot water, taking care not to let the bowl touch the water. Do not overheat the chocolate or it will separate.
Spoon the Mascarpone and fromage frais into a large bowl and whisk together until smooth.
Add the eggs and sugar and whisk again before adding the melted chocolate and Baileys. Add the raisins and toasted hazelnuts if desired.
Pour the mixture into the tin, smoothing it with the back of a spoon, and bake in the centre of the oven for 1¼ hours. After that turn the oven off but leave the cheesecake inside until it is completely cold—this will prevent it from cracking.
Melt the chocolate as before and spread on a large plate, to form a 6 inch/15 cm circle. Chill in the fridge for 45 minutes.
Using a cheese slicer or a sharp knife, drag across the surface of the chocolate to form curls or shavings.

TO SERVE
Sprinkle the surface of the cheesecake with chocolate curls or shavings, dust with a sprinkling of cocoa powder and serve in slices with crème fraîche or cream.

Icon at the Baileys Centre
Leopardstown, County Dublin

Conrad Gallagher
Peacock Alley

Some people are born to music or mathematics; Conrad Gallagher was born to cook. He started in his mother's kitchen in Donegal, and went on to casual jobs in the local hotel by the age of eleven. After working in great restaurants in Paris, Monaco and New York, he opened his first restaurant in Dublin at the age of 24. His cooking pays homage to Mediterranean and Pacific cuisines, but it also reflects an international style, one that deliberately rejects the influences of the Big House and the Ascendancy.

BAILEYS IRISH CREAM TRUFFLES

MAKES 25–30 TRUFFLES

2oz/50 g caster/superfine sugar
2 egg yolks
5 oz/125 g good quality dark/semi-sweet chocolate, grated
3 fl oz/75 ml single/light cream
2 tablespoons Baileys
1 tablespoon cocoa powder for dusting

Whisk the sugar and eggs together until pale. Place over a pan of barely simmering water and stir until the mixture coats the back of a spoon.

Place the chocolate in a heatproof bowl. Bring the cream to the boil and pour on to the chocolate. Stir until the chocolate has melted.

Mix the chocolate and egg mixtures thoroughly together.

Add the Baileys, cool and then place in the freezer to set—about 30 minutes.

When set remove from the freezer and roll teasponfuls of the mixture into ball shapes. Coat lightly with sifted cocoa powder. Refrigerate or freeze until ready to serve.

The truffles will keep for 2–3 days in the refrigerator and for up to 1 week in the freezer.

Peacock Alley
Fitzwilliam Hotel, Stephen's Green, Dublin

INDEX TO DRINKS AND FOOD

INDEX TO DRINKS